PLAY THE PIANO DRUNK LIKE A PERCUSSION INSTRUMENT UNTIL THE FINGERS BEGIN TO BLEED A BIT

CHARLES BUKOWSKI

BY CHARLES BUKOWSKI

The Days Run Away Like Wild Horses Over the Hills (1969)
Post Office (1971)
Mockingbird Wish Me Luck (1972)
South of No North (1973)
Burning in Water, Drowning in Flame: Selected Poems 1955–1973 (1974)
Factotum (1975)
Love Is a Dog from Hell: Poems 1974–1977 (1977)
Women (1978)
You Kissed Lilly (1978)
*Play the piano drunk Like a percussion Instrument Until the fingers begin to bleed
   a bit* (1979)
Shakespeare Never Did This (1979)
Dangling in the Tournefortia (1981)
Ham on Rye (1982)
Bring Me Your Love (1983)
Hot Water Music (1983)
There's No Business (1984)
War All the Time: Poems 1981–1984 (1984)
You Get So Alone At Times That It Just Makes Sense (1986)
The Movie: "Barfly" (1987)
The Roominghouse Madrigals: Early Selected Poems 1946–1966 (1988)
Hollywood (1989)
Septuagenarian Stew: Stories & Poems (1990)
The Last Night of the Earth Poems (1992)
Screams from the Balcony: Selected Letters 1960–1970 (Volume 1) (1993)
Pulp (1994)
Living on Luck: Selected Letters 1960s–1970s (Volume 2) (1995)
Betting on the Muse: Poems & Stories (1996)
Bone Palace Ballet: New Poems (1997)
The Captain Is Out to Lunch and the Sailors Have Taken Over the Ship (1998)
Reach for the Sun: Selected Letters 1978–1994 (Volume 3) (1999)
What Matters Most Is How Well You Walk Through the Fire: New Poems (1999)
Open All Night: New Poems (2000)
*Beerspit Night and Cursing: The Correspondence of Charles Bukowski &
   Sheri Martinelli* (2001)
The Night Torn Mad with Footsteps: New Poems (2001)
Sifting Through the Madness for the Word, the Line, the Way: New Poems (2002)

CHARLES BUKOWSKI

PLAY THE PIANO DRUNK LIKE A PERCUSSION INSTRUMENT UNTIL THE FINGERS BEGIN TO BLEED A BIT

ecco

An Imprint of HarperCollinsPublishers

HarperCollins books may be purchased for educational, business, or sales promotional use. For information please write: Special Markets Department, HarperCollins Publishers Inc., 10 East 53rd Street, New York, NY 10022.

ACKNOWLEDGMENTS

Grateful acknowledgment is made to the following magazines where some of these poems originally appeared: *Blitz, The Goodly Company, Hearse, Midwest, Ontario Review, The Other, Target* and *Wormwood Review*. Thanks also to Capra Press which originally published some of these poems as a chapbook called *Fire Station*.

First Ecco edition 2003.

Library of Congress Cataloging-in-Publication Data

ISBN 0-87685-437-4 (PAPER EDITION)

06 07 FOLIO/RRD 10 9 8 7 6

for Linda Lee Beighle,
the best

waiting
in a life full of little stories
for a death to come

TABLE OF CONTENTS

PLAY THE PIANO DRUNK
LIKE A PERCUSSION INSTRUMENT
UNTIL THE FINGERS BEGIN TO BLEED A BIT

tough company

poems like gunslingers
sit around and
shoot holes in my windows
chew on my toilet paper
read the race results
take the phone off the
hook.

poems like gunslingers
ask me
what the hell my game is,
and
would I like to
shoot it out?

take it easy, I say,
the race is not to
the swift.

the poem sitting at the
south end of the couch
draws
says
balls off for that
one!

take it easy, pardner, I
have plans for
you.

plans, huh? what
plans?

The New Yorker,
pard.

he puts his iron
away.

the poem sitting in the
chair near the door
stretches
looks at me:
you know, fat boy, you
been pretty lazy
lately.

fuck off
I say
who's running this
game?

we're running this
game
say all the
gunslingers
drawing iron:
get
with it!

so
here you
are:

this poem
was the one
who was sitting
on top of the
refrigerator
flipping
beercaps.

and now
I've got him
out of the way

and all the others
are sitting around pointing
their weapons at me and
saying:

I'm next, I'm next, I'm
next!

I suppose that when
I die
the leftovers
will jump some other
poor
son of a bitch.

12-24-78

I suck on this beer
in my kitchen
and think about
cleaning my fingernails
and shaving
as I listen to the
classical radio
station.
they play holiday
music.
I prefer to hear Christmas
music in July
while I am being threatened
with death by
a woman.
that's
when I need it—
that's
when I need
Bing Crosby and the
elves and
some fast
reindeer.

now I sit here
listening to this
slop in
season—it's such
a sugar tit—
I'd rather play a game of
ping-pong with
the risen ghost
of Hitler.

amateur drunks run their cheerful
cars into each other
the ambulances sing to each
other outside.

an ideal

the Waxmans, she said,
he starved,
all these builders wanted to
buy him;
he worked in Paris in London and
even in Africa,
he had his own
concept of
design. . .

what the fuck? I said,
a starving architect,
eh?

yes, yes, he starved *and* his
wife *and* his children
but he was true to
his ideals.

a starving architect,
eh?

yes, he finally came through,
I saw him and his wife last
Wednesday night, the Waxmans. . .
would you care to meet
them?

tell him, I said, to stick 3 fingers up
his ass
and flick-off.

you're always so fucking nasty, she said,
knocking over her tall-stemmed
glass of scotch and
water.

uh huh, I said, in honor of
the dead.

leaning on wood

there are 4 or 5 guys at the
racetrack bar.

there is a mirror behind the
bar.

the reflections are not
kind

of the 4 or 5 guys at the
racetrack bar.

there are many bottles at the
racetrack bar.

we order different drinks.

there is a mirror behind the
bar.

the reflections are not
kind.

"it don't take brains to beat
the horses, it just takes money
and guts."

our reflections are not
kind.

the clouds are outside.
the sun is outside.
the horses are warming up outside.

we stand at the racetrack
bar.

"I've been playing the races for
40 years and I still can't beat
them."

"you can play the races for another
40 years and you still won't beat
them."

the bartender doesn't like
us.
the 5 minute warning buzzer
sounds.

we finish our drinks and
turn away to make our
bets.

our reflections look better
as we walk away:
you can't see our
faces.

4 or 5 guys from the racetrack
bar.

what shit. nobody
wins. ask
Caesar.

the souls of dead animals

after the slaughterhouse
there was a bar around the corner
and I sat in there
and watched the sun go down
through the window,
a window that overlooked a lot
full of tall dry weeds.

I never showered with the boys at the
plant
after work
so I smelled of sweat and
blood.
the smell of sweat lessens after a
while
but the blood-smell begins to fulminate
and gain power.

I smoked cigarettes and drank beer
until I felt good enough to
board the bus
with the souls of all those dead
animals riding with
me;
heads would turn slightly
women would rise and move away from
me.

when I got off the bus
I only had a block to walk
and one stairway up to my
room
where I'd turn on my radio and
light a cigarette
and nobody minded me
at all.

another argument

she had an uncle who sniffed her
panties by
firelight while eating
crackerjack and
muffins with honey,
she sat across from me
in that Chinese place
the drinks kept coming and she
talked about Matisse, Iranian
coins, fingerbowls at Cambridge, Pound
at Salerno, Plato at
Madagascar, the death of
Schopenhauer, and the times she and
I had been together and
ebullient.

drunk in the afternoon
I knew she had kept me too long
and when I got back to the *other*
she was
raving
underprivileged
pissed and
bloody unorthodox burning
mad.

then she said it didn't matter anymore
and I felt like saying
what do you mean it doesn't matter anymore?
how can you say it about anything, least of
all us? where are your eyes and your feet and
your head? if the thin blue marching of troops is
correct, we are all about to be
murdered.

the red porsche

it feels good
to be driven about in a red
porsche
by a woman better-
read than I
am.
it feels good
to be driven about in a red
porsche
by a woman who can explain
things about
classical
music to
me.

it feels good
to be driven about in a red
porsche
by a woman who buys
things for my refrigerator
and my
kitchen:
cherries, plums, lettuce, celery,
green onions, brown onions,
eggs, muffins, long
chilis, brown sugar,
Italian seasoning, oregano, white
wine vinegar, pompeian olive oil
and red
radishes.

I like being driven about
in a red porsche
while I smoke cigarettes in
gentle languor.

I'm lucky. I've always been
lucky:
even when I was starving to death
the bands were playing for
me.
but the red porsche is very nice
and she is
too, and
I've learned to feel good when
I feel good.

it's better to be driven around in a
red porsche
than to own
one. the luck of the fool is
inviolate.

some picnic

which reminds me
I shacked with Jane for 7 years
she was a drunk
I loved her

my parents hated her
I hated my parents
it made a nice
foursome

one day we went on a picnic
together
up in the hills
and we played cards and drank beer and
ate potato salad and weenies

they talked to her as if she were a living person
at last

everybody laughed
I didn't laugh.

later at my place
over the whiskey
I said to her,
I don't like them
but it's good they treated you
nice.

you damn fool, she said,
don't you see?

see what?

they keep looking at my beer-belly,
they think I'm
pregnant.

oh, I said, well here's to our beautiful
child.

here's to our beautiful child,
she said.

we drank them down.

the drill

our marriage book, it
says.
I look through it.
they lasted ten years.
they were young once.
now I sleep in her bed.
he phones her:
"I want my drill back.
have it ready.
I'll pick the children up at
ten."
when he arrives he waits outside
the door.
his children leave with
him.
she comes back to bed
and I stretch a leg out
place it against hers.
I was young once too.
human relationships simply aren't
durable.
I think back to the women in
my life.
they seem non-existent.

"did he get his drill?" I ask.

"yes, he got his drill."

I wonder if I'll ever have to come
back for my bermuda
shorts and my record album
by *The Academy of St. Martin in the
Fields*? I suppose I
will.

40,000 flies

torn by a temporary wind
we come back together again

check walls and ceilings for cracks and
the eternal spiders

wonder if there will be one more
woman

now
40,000 flies running the arms of my
soul
singing
*I met a million dollar baby in a
5 and 10 cent
store*

arms of my soul?
flies?
singing?

what kind of shit is
this?

it's so easy to be a poet
and so hard to be
a man.

the strangest thing

I was sitting in a chair
in the dark
when horrible sounds of torture
and fear
began in the brush
outside of my window.
it was obviously not a male cat
and a female cat
but a male and a male
and from the sound
one appeared to be much larger
and was attacking with the intent to
kill.
then it stopped.

then it began again
worse this time;
the sounds were so terrible
that I was unable to
move.

then the sounds stopped.

I got up from my chair
went to bed and
slept.

I had a dream. this small grey and white
cat came to me in my dream
and it was very
sad. it spoke to me,
it said:
"look what the other cat did to me."
and it rested in my lap
and I saw the slashes and

the raw flesh. then it
jumped off my lap.

then that was all.

I awakened at 8:45 p.m.
put on my clothes and walked outside
and looked around.

there was nothing
there.

I walked back inside and
dropped two eggs
into a pot of water
and turned up the
flame.

... the drawing is poor and I know little of the plot:
a man with a stable, world-earned face and the necktie of
respectability, and a satisfied pipe; and his wife—
signified by the quick ink of black hair (just ever so
tousled with having *babies* and guiding them safely through
the falls) : there is a grandmother who sits somewhat like
a flowerpot: allotted an earned space but not really
useful; and a couple of smiling, knee-climbing gamins
two little Jung and Adlers
full of moot, black-type questions,
and, of course,
a young girl troubled with young loves
(they take these things so much more *seriously* than the
young men who
go behind the barn);
and there *is* a young man—her, I presume barn-wise, brother
with this great tundra, this *shield* of black hair;
he is horribly healthy
and dressed in the latest in sport shirts
in the best barn-wise manner;
this big ... brother (16? 17? 18? God wot?)
is usually (when I read this, which is not very often)
leaning forward over the car seat
 (he sits in the back, like the author)
and makes some ... comment on LIFE, capital all-the-way LIFE
that is so VERY true
that it just ... upsets *every*body
except the poor kiddies who don't know what the hell it's
all about in spite of their Jung and Adler
and they just ride along round-eyed and sucking at their
lollypops all up in the pretty pure white clouds;
but, lo, the headman grinds his pipe grey-faced against this
sporty truth that old men let lie like overgrown
gas-meter covers; and the mother (wife wot?) draws down
a long black eyebrow and one more strand of hair becomes
unattached in the cool long struggle; and

Grandma, oh, I don't know—
by then I have looked away; but I remember the girl,
the young girl with young loves
is always *especially* angry
because the back of the barn has been blamed on her...
locked with René the Frenchman, the struggling ... painter or
wot?
nobody wants to face it but this ... fat ... sports-wear shirt
character (who is *really* a nice strong boy who will really
be O.K. some day) keeps bringing the cow out from behind the
    barn
with the bull; but he is young
and laughs
and all somehow bear up;
but best is his ... *explanation* of it all,
of the cow and the bull,
with the inherent and instinctive ... wiseness of his
youth;
the *explanation* usually comes in the morning
over the breakfast table—
before all this sickly struggling ordinary mess of common ...
humanity has had a chance
to seat itself
the healthy white ... face laughs and tells it all;
he's been sitting there waiting to tell it all,
he's been sitting there with the little ... twins (or wot?)
as they spill porridge so cutely with their little spoons,
this big ... happy oaf who's never had a toothache
has been sitting waiting the entrance of his elders
(Granny who must put in her teeth, and Papa who is worried
about the office, and Mama who isn't exactly straightened out
yet; and the young girl who loves with faith, anger and ...
purity) in they come
and he *throws* out an arm
and tilting his healthy ... carcass madly back in the chair
before the sun-pure kitchen curtains
and the little lovable, struggling bungling group
he says his great say,
and in the balloon above his head are the words

and by the twisted agony of the faces
I am led to believe *something* has been said,
but I read again
looking carefully at the great happy spewing oaf's face
the brown great deepness of the eyes
and the young girl's teeth pushed out sour as if she had
bitten into some lemon of truth,
but there is something wrong
there is some mistake
because the sheet of paper I hold
slants and angles in the electric light
into the open dizziness of my dome
and it huddles and curls itself into a puffy knot
and pushes at the back of my eyes
and pulls my nerves taut-thin from toe to hair-line
and I know then that
the great spewing oaf has said
nothing nothing nothing nothing nothing nothing nothing
nothing nothing nothing nothing nothing nothing nothing
nothing nothing nothing nothing nothing nothing nothing
and now,
on the rug
under the chair
I can see the comic section
folded in half,
I can see the black and white lines
and some faces I don't care to discern;
but a thin illness overcomes me
at the sight of this portion of paper
and I look away
and try not to think
that much of our living life
is true to the little paper faces
that stare up from our feet
and grin and jump and gesture,
to be wrapped in tomorrow's garbage
and thrown away.

2 flies

The flies are angry bits of
life;
why are they so angry?
it seems they want more,
it seems almost as if they
are angry
that they are flies;
it is not my fault;
I sit in the room
with them
and they taunt me
with their agony;
it is as if they were
loose chunks of soul
left out of somewhere;
I try to read a paper
but they will not let me
be;
one seems to go in half-circles
high along the wall,
throwing a miserable sound
upon my head;
the other one, the smaller one
stays near and teases my hand,
saying nothing,
rising, dropping
crawling near;
what god puts these
lost things upon me?
other men suffer dictates of
empire, tragic love . . .
I suffer
insects . . .
I wave at the little one
which only seems to revive
his impulse to challenge:

he circles swifter,
nearer, even making
a fly-sound,
and one above
catching a sense of the new
whirling, he too, in excitement,
speeds his flight,
drops down suddenly
in a cuff of noise
and they join
in circling my hand,
strumming the base
of the lampshade
until some man-thing
in me
will take no more
unholiness
and I strike
with the rolled-up paper—
missing!—
striking,
striking,
they break in discord,
some message lost between them,
and I get the big one
first, and he kicks on his back
flicking his legs
like an angry whore,
and I come down again
with my paper club
and he is a smear
of fly-ugliness;
the little one circles high
now, quiet and swift,
almost invisible;
he does not come near
my hand again;
he is tamed and
inaccessible; I leave

him be, he leaves me
be;
the paper, of course,
is ruined;
something has happened,
something has soiled my
day,
sometimes it does not
take a man
or a woman,
only something alive;
I sit and watch
the small one;
we are woven together
in the air
and the living;
it is late
for both of us.

of course it is nonsense to try to patch up an
old poem while drinking a warm beer
on a Sunday afternoon; it is better to simply
exist through the end of a cigarette;
the people are listless and although this is a
poor term of description
Gershwin is on the radio
banging and praying to get out;
I have read the newspapers,
carefully noting the suicides,
I have also carefully noted
the green of some tree
like a nature poet on his last cup,
and
bang bang
there they go outside;
new children, some of them getting ready
to sit here, and do as I am doing—
warm beer, dead Gershwin,
getting fat around the middle,
disbelieving the starving years,
Atlanta frozen like God's head
holding an apple in the window,
but we are all finally tricked and
slapped to death
like lovers' vows, bargained
out of any gain,
and the radio is finished
and the phone rings and a female says,
"I am free tonight;" well, she is not much
but I am not much either;
in adolescent fire I once thought I could ride
a horse through the streets of anywhere,
but they quickly shot this horse from under,
"Ya got cigarettes?" she asks. "Yes," I say,
"I got cigarettes." "Matches?" she asks.

"Enough matches to burn Rome." "Whiskey?"
"Enough whiskey for a Mississippi River
of pain." "You drunk?" "Not yet."
She'll be over: perfect: a fig
leaf and a small club, and
I look at the poem I am trying to work with:

> *I say that*
> *the backalleys will arrive upon*
> *the bloodyapes*
> *as noon arrives upon the Salinas*
> *fieldhands ....*

bullshit. I rip the page once, twice,
three times, then check for matches and
icecubes, hot and cold,
with some men their conversation is better than
their creation
and with other men
it's a woman
almost any woman
that is their Rodin among park benches;
bird down in road awaiting rats and wheels
I know that I have deserted you,
the icecubes pile like fool's gold
in the pitcher
and now they are playing
Alex Scriabin
which is a little better
but not much
for me.

fire station

(For Jane, with love)

we came out of the bar
because we were out of money
but we had a couple of wine bottles
in the room.

it was about 4 in the afternoon
and we passed a fire station
and she started to go
crazy:

"a FIRE STATION! oh, I just love
FIRE engines, they're so red and
all! let's go in!"

I followed her on
in. "FIRE ENGINES!" she screamed
wobbling her big
ass.

she was already trying to climb into
one, pulling her skirt up to her
waist, trying to jacknife up into the
seat.

"here, here, lemme help ya!" a fireman ran
up.

another fireman walked up to
me: "our citizens are always welcome,"
he told
me.

the other guy was up in the seat with
her. "you got one of those big THINGS?"

she asked him. "oh, hahaha!, I mean one of
those big HELMETS!"

"I've got a big helmet too," he told
her.

"oh, hahaha!"

"you play cards?" I asked *my*
fireman. I had 43 cents and nothing but
time.

"come on in back," he
said. "of course, we don't gamble.
it's against the
rules."

"I understand," I told
him.

I had run my 43 cents up to a
dollar ninety
when I saw her going upstairs with
her fireman.

"he's gonna show me their sleeping
quarters," she told
me.

"I understand," I told
her.

when her fireman slid down the pole
ten minutes later
I nodded him
over.

"that'll be 5
dollars."

"5 dollars for
that?"

"we wouldn't want a scandal, would
we? we both might lose our
jobs. of course, I'm not
working."

he gave me the
5.

"sit down, you might get it
back."

"whatcha playing?"
"blackjack."

"gambling's against the
law."

"anything interesting is. besides,
you see any money on the
table?"
he sat down.

that made 5 of
us.

"how was it Harry?" somebody asked
him.

"not bad, not
bad."

the other guy went on
upstairs.

they were bad players really.
they didn't bother to memorize the

deck. they didn't know whether the
high numbers or low numbers were left. and basically they hit too
  high,
didn't hold low
enough.

when the other guy came down
he gave me a
five.

"how was it, Marty?"
"not bad. she's got . . . some fine
movements."

"hit me!" I said. "nice clean girl. I
ride it myself."

nobody said
anything.

"any big fires lately?" I
asked.

"naw. nothin'
much."

"you guys need
exercise. hit me
again!"

a big red-headed kid who had been shining an
engine
threw down his rag and
went upstairs.

when he came down he threw me a
five.

41

when the 4th guy came down I gave him
3 fives for a
twenty.

I don't know how many firemen
were in the building or where they
were. I figured a few had slipped by me
but I was a good
sport.

it was getting dark outside
when the alarm
rang.

they started running around.
guys came sliding down the
pole.

then she came sliding down the
pole. she was good with the
pole. a real woman. nothing but guts
and
ass.

"let's go," I told
her.

she stood there waving goodbye to the
firemen but they didn't seem
much interested
any more.

"let's go back to the
bar," I told
her.

"ooh, you got
money?"

"I found some I didn't know I
had ..."

we sat at the end of the bar
with whiskey and beer
chaser.
"I sure got a good
sleep."

"sure, baby, you need your
sleep."

"look at that sailor looking at me!
he must think I'm a ... a ..."

"naw, he don't think that. relax, you've got
class, real class. sometimes you remind me of an
opera singer. you know, one of those prima d's.
your class shows all over
you. drink
up."

I ordered 2
more.

"you know, daddy, you're the only man I
LOVE! I mean, really ... LOVE! ya
know?"

"sure I know. sometimes I think I am a king
in spite of myself."

"yeah. yeah. *that's* what I mean, somethin' like
that."

I had to go to the urinal. when I came back
the sailor was sitting in my
seat. she had her leg up against his and
he was talking.

43

I walked over and got in a dart game with
Harry the Horse and the corner
newsboy.

an argument over *Marshal Foch*

Foch was a great soldier, he said, Marshal Foch;
listen, I said, if you don't keep it clean
I'll have to slap you across the face with
a wet towel.

I'll write the governor, he said.
the governor is my uncle, I said.

Marshal Foch was my
grandfather, he said.

I warned you, I said. I'm a
gentleman.

And I'm a Foch, he said.
that did it. I slapped him with a wet towel.

he grabbed the phone.
governor's mansion, he said.

I slapped a wet rubber glove down
his mouth and cut the wire.

outside the crickets were chirping like
mad: Foch, Foch, Foch, Foch!
they chirped.

I got out my sub-machine gun and blasted
the devils
but there were so many of them
I had to give up.

I pulled the wet rubber glove out.
I surrender, I said, it's too much:
I can't change the world.

all the so-called ladies in the room
applauded.

he stood up and bowed gallantly as
outside the crickets chirped.

I put on my hat
and stalked out. I still maintain
the French are weak
and no
wonder.

40 cigarettes

I smoked 2 packs of cigarettes today and
my tongue feels like a
caterpillar trying to get out for
rainwater
somebody is working over
Pictures at an Exhibition
while tiny pimples of sweat
work their way down my
fat sides.
too sick today and told the man
over the phone
it was stomach pains.
the pains in the ass too and
the soul?
the gophers are underground
staring at pictures on mudwalls
machineguns are mounted in the
windows.
40 cigarettes.
what's walking around
chewing grass,
4 legs, no
hands?
it's not the
politburo.
it could be a
donkey. how'd you like to be in a
donkey's head for a
while? your body in a donkey's
body? you'd only last
ten minutes
they'd have to let you
out
you'd be so
scared
but who's going to

let you out of that
dismal bluepurple notion
of what you are
now? and I'm the one who's
scared.

a killer gets ready

he was a good one
say 18, 19,
a marine
and everytime
a woman came down the train aisle
he seemed to stand up
so I couldn't see
her
and the woman smiled at him

but I didn't smile
at him

he kept looking at himself in the
train window
and standing up and taking off his
coat and then standing up
and putting it back
on

he polished his belt buckle with a
delighted vigor

and his neck was red and
his face was red and his eyes were a
pretty blue

but I didn't like
him

and everytime I went to the can
he was either in one of the cans
or he was in front of one of the mirrors
combing his hair or
shaving

and he was always walking up and down the
aisles
or drinking water
I watched his Adam's apple juggle the water
down

he was always in my
eyes

but we never spoke
and I remembered all the other trains
all the other buses
all the other wars

he got off at Pasadena
vainer than any woman
he got off at Pasadena
proud and
dead

the rest of the trainride—
8 or 10 miles—
was perfect.

I love you

I opened the door of this shanty and there she lay
there she lay
my love
across the back of a man in a dirty undershirt.
I was rough tough easy-with-money-Charley (that's me)
and I awakened both of them
like God
and when she was awake
she started screaming, "Hank, Hank!" (that's my other name)
"take me away from this son of a bitch!
I hate him I love you!"

of course, I was wise enough not to believe any of
this and I sat down and said,
"I need a drink, my head hurts and I need a
drink."

this is the way love works, you see, and then we all sat there
drinking the whiskey and I was
perfectly satisfied
and then he reached over and handed me a five,
"that's all that's left of what she took, that's all that's left
of what she took from you."

I was no golden-winged angel ripped up through
boxtops
I took the five and left them in there
and I walked up the alley
to Alvarado street
and I turned in left
at the first
bar.

a little atomic bomb

o, just give me a little atomic bomb
not too much
just a little
enough to kill a horse in the street
but there aren't any horses in the street

well, enough to knock the flowers from a bowl
but I don't see any
flowers in a
bowl

enough then
to frighten my love
but I don't have any
love

well
give me an atomic bomb then
to scrub in my bathtub
like a dirty and lovable child

(I've got a bathtub)

just a little atomic bomb, general,
with pugnose
pink ears
smelling like underclothes in
July

do you think I'm crazy?
I think you're crazy
too
so the way you think:
send me one before somebody else
does.

the egg

he's 17.
mother, he said, how do I crack an
egg?

all right, she said to me, you don't have to
sit there looking like that.

oh, mother, he said, you broke the yoke.
I can't eat a broken yoke.

all right, she said to me, you're so tough,
you've been in the slaughterhouses, factories,
the jails, you're so god damned tough,
but all people don't have to be like you,
that doesn't make everybody else wrong and you
right.

mother, he said, can you bring me some cokes
when you come home from work?

look, Raleigh, she said, can't you get the cokes
on your bike, I'm tired after
work.

but, mama, there's a hill.

what hill, Raleigh?

there's a hill,
it's there and I have to peddle over
it.

all right, she said to me, you think you're so
god damned tough. you worked on a railroad track
gang, I hear about it every time you get drunk:
"I worked on a railroad track gang."

well, I said, I did.

I mean, what difference does it make?
everybody has to work somewhere.

mama, said the kid, will you bring me those
cokes?

I really like the kid. I think he's very
gentle. and once he learns how to crack an
egg he may do some
unusual things. meanwhile
I sleep with his mother
and try to stay out of
arguments.

the knifer

you knifed me, he said, you told *Pink Eagle*
not to publish me.
oh hell, Manny, I said, get off it.

these poets are very sensitive
they have more sensitivity than talent,
I don't know what to do with them.

just tonight the phone rang and
it was Bagatelli and Bagatelli said
Clarsten phoned and Clarsten was pissed
because we hadn't mailed him the
anthology, and Clarsten blamed me
for not mailing the anthology
and furthermore Clarsten
claimed I was trying to do him
in, and he was very
angry. so said
Bagatelli.

you know, I'm really beginning to feel like
a literary power
I just lean back in my chair and roll cigarettes
and stare at the walls
and I am given credit for the life and death of
poetic careers.
at least I'm given credit for the
death part.

actually these boys are dying off without my
help. The sun has gone behind the cloud.
I have nothing to do with the workings.
I smoke Prince Albert, drink Schlitz
and copulate whenever possible. believe in my
innocence and I might consider
yours.

the ladies of summer

the ladies of summer will die like the rose
and the lie

the ladies of summer will love
so long as the price is not
forever

the ladies of summer
might love anybody;
they might even love you
as long as summer
lasts

yet winter will come to them
too

white snow and
a cold freezing
and faces so ugly
that even death
will turn away—
wince—
before taking
them.

I'm in love

she's young, she said,
but look at me,
I have pretty ankles,
and look at my wrists, I have pretty
wrists
o my god,
I thought it was all working,
and now it's her again,
every time she phones you go crazy,
you told me it was over
you told me it was finished,
listen, I've lived long enough to become a
good woman,
why do you need a bad woman?
you need to be tortured, don't you?
you think life is rotten if somebody treats you
rotten it all fits,
doesn't it?
tell me, is that it? do you want to be treated like a
piece of shit?
and my son, my son was going to meet you.
I told my son
and I dropped all my lovers.
I stood up in a cafe and screamed
I'M IN LOVE,
and now you've made a fool of me . . .

I'm sorry, I said, I'm really sorry.

hold me, she said, will you please hold me?

I've never been in one of these things before, I said,
these triangles . . .

she got up and lit a cigarette, she was trembling all
over. she paced up and down, wild and crazy. she had

57

a small body. her arms were thin, very thin and when
she screamed and started beating me I held her
wrists and then I got it through the eyes: hatred,
centuries deep and true. I was wrong and graceless and
sick. all the things I had learned had been wasted.
there was no living creature as foul as I
and all my poems were
false.

the apple

this is not just an apple
this is an experience
red green yellow
with underlying pits of white
wet with cold water
I bite into it
christ, a white doorway . . .

another bite
chewing
while thinking of an old witch
choking to death on an apple skin—
a childhood story.

I bite deeply
chew and swallow

there is a feeling of waterfalls
and endlessness

there is a mixture of electricity and
hope.

yet now
halfway through the apple
some depressive feelings begin

it's ending
I'm working toward the core
afraid of seeds and stems

there's a funeral march beginning in Venice,
a dark old man has died after a lifetime of pain

I throw away the apple early
as a girl in a white dress walks by my window

followed by a boy half her size
in blue pants and striped
shirt

I leave off a small belch
and stare at a dirty
ashtray.

the violin player

he was in the upper grandstand
at the end
where they made their stretch moves
after coming off the curve.

he was a small man
pink, bald, fat
in his 60's.

he was playing a violin
he was playing classical music on
his violin
and the horseplayers ignored him.

Banker Agent won the first race
and he played his violin.

Can Fly won the 3rd race and
he continued to play his violin.

I went to get a coffee and when I came back
he was still playing, and he was still playing
after Boomerang won the 4th.

nobody stopped him
nobody asked him what he was doing
nobody applauded.

after Pawee won the 5th
he continued
the music falling over the edge of the
grandstand and into the
wind and sun.

Stars and Stripes won the 6th
and he played some more

and Staunch Hope got up on the inside
to take the 7th
and the violin player worked away
and when Lucky Mike won at 4 to 5 in the 8th
he was still making music.

after Dumpty's Goddess took the last
and they began their long slow walk to their cars
beaten and broke again
the violin player continued
sending his music after them
and I sat there listening
we were both alone up there and
when he finished I applauded.
the violin player stood up
faced me and bowed.
then he put his fiddle in the case
got up and walked down the stairway.

I allowed him a few minutes
and then I got up
and began the long slow walk to my car.
it was getting into evening.

5 dollars

I am dying of sadness and alcohol
he said to me over the bottle
on a soft Thursday afternoon
in an old hotel room by the train depot.

I have, he went on, betrayed myself with
belief, deluded myself with love
tricked myself with sex.

the bottle is damned faithful, he said,
the bottle will not lie.

meat is cut as roses are cut
men die as dogs die
love dies like dogs die,
he said.

listen, Ronny, I said,
lend me 5 dollars.

love needs too much help, he said.
hate takes care of itself.

just 5 dollars, Ronny.

hate contains truth. beauty is a facade.

I'll pay you back in a week.

stick with the thorn
stick with the bottle
stick with the voices of old men in hotel rooms.

I ain't had a decent meal, Ronny, for a
couple of days.

stick with the laughter and horror of death.
keep the butterfat out.
get lean, get ready.

something in my gut, Ronny, I'll be able
to face it.

to die alone and ready and unsurprised,
that's the trick.

Ronny, listen—

that majestic weeping you hear
will not be for
us.

I suppose not, Ronny.

the lies of centuries, the lies of love,
the lies of Socrates and Blake and Christ
will be your bedmates and tombstones
in a death that will never end.

Ronny, my poems came back from the
New York Quarterly.

that is why they weep,
without knowing.

is that what all that noise is, I said,
my god shit.

cooperation

she means well.
play the piano
she says
it's not good for you
not to write.

she's going for a walk
on the island
or a boatride.
I believe she's taken a modern novel
and her reading glasses.

I sit at the window
with her electric typewriter
and watch young girls' asses
which are attached to
young girls.

the final decadence.

I have 20 published books
and 6 cans of beer.

the tourists bob up and down in the water
the tourists walk and talk and take
photographs and
drink soft drinks.

it's not good for me not to
write.
she's in a boat now, a
sightseeing tour
and she's thinking, looking
at the waves—
"it's 2:30 p.m.
he must be writing

it's not good for him not to write.
tonight there will be other things to do.
I hope he doesn't drink
too much beer. he's a much better
lover than Robert was
and the sea is beautiful."

the night I was going to die

the night I was going to die
I was sweating on the bed
and I could hear the crickets
and there was a cat fight outside
and I could feel my soul dropping down through the
mattress
and just before it hit the floor I jumped up
I was almost too weak to walk
but I walked around and turned on all the lights
then made it back to the bed
and again my soul dropped down through the mattress
and I leaped up
just before it hit the floor
I walked around and I turned on all the lights
and then I went back to bed
and down it dropped again and
I was up
turning on all the lights

I had a 7 year old daughter
and I felt sure she didn't want me dead
otherwise it wouldn't have
mattered

but all that night
nobody phoned
nobody came by with a beer
my girlfriend didn't phone
all I could hear were the crickets and it was
hot
and I kept working at it
getting up and down
until the first of the sun came through the window
through the bushes
and then I got on the bed
and the soul stayed

inside at last and
I slept.
now people come by
beating on the doors and windows
the phone rings
the phone rings again and again
I get great letters in the mail
hate letters and love letters.
everything is the same again.

2347 *Duane*

there's this blue baby and she's sucking a
blue breast under a green vine that has
grown from the ceiling,
and further to the right
there's a light brown girl
against a dark brown background
and she's leaning out over a chair looking
pensive, I suppose.
my cigarette just went out
there are never any matches around here
and I get up and go into the kitchen
and light it on a 30 year old stove.
I get back without accident.
now behind me on a pink chair
is a large old-fashioned shears.
it is 15 minutes past midnight
and the hook is on the door
and over the tall twisted lamp by the bed
is a red floppy hat that is used as a lampshade
and a small dog growls at the tall cold sky outside.
there are two mattresses on the floor
and I have slept on one of those mattresses
many nights.
they say they are going to bulldoze this place
which is owned by a Japanese wrestler called Fuji.
I don't see how it can be replaced with anything better.

she fixed the bathtub faucet and the faucet in the sink
tonight. she can't roll a cigarette but she keeps the
plumbing bills down.
we ate some Col. Sanders chicken with coleslaw, mashed spuds,
gravy and biscuits.
it's 23 minutes past midnight
and they are going to bulldoze this place,
I don't mean tomorrow, I mean soon,
and the small dog growls at the sky again

and my cigarette is out again;
the love on that one mattress near the door,
the sex and the arguments and the dreams and the
conversations,
that bulldozer is going to come up missing there,
and even when it knocks down the trees and the crapper
and eats holes in the dirt driveway
it's not going to get it all,
and when I drive by in 6 months and see the highrise
filled with 50 people with good stable incomes,
I will still remember the blue baby sucking the blue breast,
the vine through the roof, the brown girl,
the leaky faucets, the spiders and the termites,
the grey and yellow paint, the tablecloth over the front
window, and that mattress near the door.

a radio with guts

it was on the 2nd floor on Coronado Street
I used to get drunk
and throw the radio through the window
while it was playing, and, of course,
it would break the glass in the window
and the radio would sit out there on the roof
still playing
and I'd tell my woman,
"Ah, what a marvelous radio!"

the next morning I'd take the window
off the hinges
and carry it down the street
to the glass man
who would put in another pane.

I kept throwing that radio through the window
each time I got drunk
and it would sit out there on the roof
still playing—
a magic radio
a radio with guts,
and each morning I'd take the window
back to the glass man.

I don't remember how it ended exactly
though I do remember
we finally moved out.
there was a woman downstairs who worked in
the garden in her bathing suit
and her husband complained he couldn't sleep nights
because of me
so we moved out
and in the next place
I either forgot to throw the radio out the window
or I didn't feel like it
anymore.

71

I do remember missing the woman who worked in the
garden in her bathing suit,
she really dug with that trowel
and she put her behind up in the air
and I used to sit in the window
and watch the sun shine all over that thing

while the music played.

Solid State Marty

he's almost 80 and they went to
visit him the other
day. he was sitting in his chair
with a burlap rug over his
lap
and when they walked in
the first thing he said was
"Don't touch my cock!"

he had a gallon jug of
zinfandel in his
refrigerator, had just gotten off
of
5 days of
tequila.

a new $600 piano was in the center of
the room,
he'd bought it for his
son.

he's always phoning for *me* to come over
but when I do
he's very dull. he agrees with
everything I say and
then he goes to
sleep.

Solid State Marty.
when I'm not there
he does everything:
sets fire to the couch
pisses on his belly
sings the National Anthem.

he gets call girls over and
squirts them with
seltzer water, he
rips the telephone wire out
of the wall

but before he does
he telephones
Paris
Madrid
Tokyo

he beats dogs
cats
people
with his
silver crutch

he tells stories about
how he was a
matador
a boxer
a pimp
a friend of Ernie's
a friend of Picasso

but when I come over
he goes to sleep
upright in his chair
grey hair rumbling down over
the silent
dumb hawk face

his son starts talking
and then it's time
for me
to go.

interviews

young men from the underground
newspapers and the small circulation
magazines come
more and more often
to interview me—
their hair is long
they are thin
have tape recorders and
arrive with
much beer.
most
of them
manage to stay some hours and
get intoxicated.

if one of my girlfriends is around
I get her to do the
talking.
go ahead, I say, tell them the
truth about me.

then they tell what they think is
the truth.

they paint me to resemble the
idiot
which is true.

then I'm questioned:

*why did you stop writing for ten
years?*

I don't know.

*how come you didn't get into the
army?*

crazy.

can you speak German?

no.

*who are your favorite modern
writers?*

I don't know.

I seldom see the
interviews. although once one of
the young men wrote back that
my girlfriend had
kissed him
when I was in the bathroom.

you got off easy, I wrote back
and by the way
forget that shit I told you about
Dos Passos. or was it
Mailer? it's hot tonight
and half the neighborhood is
drunk. the other half is
dead.
if I have any advice about writing
poetry, it's—
don't. I'm going to send out for
some fried chicken.

buk

face of a political candidate on a street billboard

there he is:
not too many hangovers
not too many fights with women
not too many flat tires
never a thought of suicide

not more than three toothaches
never missed a meal
never in jail
never in love

7 pairs of shoes

a son in college

a car one year old

insurance policies

a very green lawn

garbage cans with tight lids

he'll be elected.

Yankee Doodle

I was young
no stomach
arms of wire
but strong

I arrived drunk at the factory
every morning
and out-worked the whole pack of them
without strain

the old guy
his name was Sully
good old Irish Sully
he fumbled with screws

and whistled the same song all day
long:

Yankee Doodle came to town
Ridin' on a pony
He stuck a feather in his hat
And called it macaroni . . .

they say he had been whistling that song
for years

I began whistling right along
with him

we whistled together for hours
him counting screws
me packing 8 foot long light fixtures into
coffin boxes

as the days went on
he began to pale and tremble
he'd miss a note now and then

I whistled on

he began to miss days

then he missed a week

next I knew
the word got out
Sully was in a hospital for an
operation

2 weeks later he came in with a cane
and his wife

he shook hands with everybody

a 40 year man

when they had the retirement party for him
I missed it
because of a terrible
hangover

after he was gone
oddly
I kept looking for him,
and I realized that he had
never hated me, that I
had only hated
him
I began drinking more
missing more days

then they let me go
too

I've never minded getting
fired but that was the one time
I felt it.

blue moon, oh bleweeww mooooon
how I adore you!

I care for you, darling, I love you,
the only reason I fucked L. is because you fucked
Z. and then I fucked R. and you fucked N.
and because you fucked N. I had to fuck
Y. But I think of you constantly, I feel you
here in my belly like a baby, love I'd call it,
no matter what happens I'd call it love, and so
you fucked C. and then before I could move
you fucked W., so then I had to fuck D. But
I want you to know that I love you, I think of you
constantly, I don't think I've ever loved anybody
like I love you.

bow wow bow wow wow
bow wow bow wow wow.

nothing is as effective
as defeat

always carry a notebook with you
wherever you go, he said,
and don't drink too much, drinking dulls
the sensibilities,
attend readings, note breath pauses,
and when *you* read
always understate
underplay, the crowd is smarter than you
might think,
and when you write something
don't send it out right away,
put it in a drawer for two weeks,
then take it out and look
at it, and revise, revise,
REVISE again and again,
tighten lines like bolts holding the span
of a 5 mile bridge,
and keep a notebook by your bed,
you will get thoughts during the night
and these thoughts will vanish and be wasted
unless you notate them.
and don't drink, any fool can
drink, we are men of
letters.

for a guy who couldn't write at all
he was about like the rest
of them: he could sure
talk about
it.

success

I had a most difficult job
starting my 14 year old car today
in 100 degree heat
I had to take the carburetor off
leap back and forth
adjusting the set-screw,
a 2 by 4 jammed against the gas pedal
to hold it down.

I got it going—after 45 minutes—
I mailed 4 letters
purchased something cool
came back
got into my place
and listened to Ives
had dreams of empire
my great white belly against
the fan.

Africa, Paris, Greece

there are these 2 women
I know who are
quite similar

almost the same
age
well-read
literary

I once slept with both of
them
but that's all
over

we're friends

they've been to Africa
Paris
Greece

here and there

fucked some famous men

one is now living with a
millionaire
some few miles
from here
goes to breakfast and
dinner with him
feeds his fish his cats and
his dog
when she gets drunk she phones
me

the other is having it
more difficult living
alone in a small apartment in
Venice (Calif.)
listening to the bongo
drums

famous men seem to want
young women

a young woman is easier
to get rid
of: they have more
places to
go

it is difficult for women who
were once beautiful
to get
old

they have to become more
intelligent (if they want to
hold their men) and do
more things
in bed and out of
bed

these 2 women I know
they're good both
in and out of
bed

and they're intelligent
intelligent enough to know
they can't come see me
and stay
more than an
hour or two

they are quite
similar

and I know
if they read this poem
they'll understand
it
just as well as they
understand
Rimbaud or Rilke

or Keats

meanwhile I have met a
young blonde from the
Fairfax district

as she looks at my paintings
on the walls
I rub the bottoms of
her feet.

the drunk tank judge

the drunk tank judge is
late like any other
judge and he is
young
well-fed
educated
spoiled and
from a good
family.

we drunks put out our cigarettes and await his
mercy.

those who couldn't make bail are
first. "guilty," they say, they all say,
"guilty."
"7 days." "14 days." "14 days and then you will be
released to the Honor Farm." "4 days." "7days."
"14 days."

"judge, these guys beat hell out of a man
in there."

"next."

"judge, they really beat hell out of me."

"next case, please."

"7 days." "14 days and then you will be released to the
Honor Farm."

the drunk tank judge is
young and
overfed. he has
eaten too many meals. he is
fat.

the bail-out drunks are
next. they put us in long lines and
he takes us
quickly. "2 days or 40 dollars." "2 days or 40
dollars." "2 days or 40 dollars." "2 days or
40 dollars."

there are 35 or
40 of us.
the courthouse is on San Fernando Road among the
junkyards.

when we go to the bailiff he
tells us,
"your bail will apply."

"what?"

"your bail will apply."

the bail is $50. the court keeps the
ten.

we walk outside and get into our
old automobiles.
most of our automobiles look worse than
the ones in the
junkyards. some of us
don't have any
automobiles. most of us are
Mexicans and poor whites.
the trainyards are across the
street. the sun is up
good.

the judge has very
smooth
delicate
skin. the judge has

fat
jowls.

we walk and we drive away from the
courthouse.

justice.

claws of paradise

wooden butterfly
baking soda smile
sawdust fly—
I love my belly
and the liquor store man
calls me,
"Mr. Schlitz."
the cashiers at the race track
scream,
"THE POET KNOWS!"
when I cash my tickets.
the ladies
in and out of bed
say they love me
as I walk by with wet
white feet.

albatross with drunken eyes
Popeye's dirt-stained shorts
bedbugs of Paris,
I have cleared the barricades
have mastered the
automobile
the hangover
the tears
but I know
the final doom
like any schoolboy viewing
the cat being crushed
by passing traffic.

my skull has an inch and a
half crack right at the
dome.
most of my teeth are
in front. I get

dizzy spells in supermarkets
spit blood when I drink
whiskey
and become saddened to
the point of
grief
when I think of all the
good women I have known
who have
dissolved
vanished
over trivialities:
trips to Pasadena,
children's picnics,
toothpaste caps down
the drain.

there is nothing to do
but drink
play the horse
bet on the poem

as the young girls
become women
and the machineguns
point toward me
crouched
behind walls thinner
than eyelids.

there's no defense
except all the errors
made.

meanwhile
I take showers
answer the phone
boil eggs

study motion and waste
and feel as good
as the next while
walking in the sun.

the loner

16 and one-half inch
neck
68 years old
lifts weights
body like a young
boy (almost)

kept his head
shaved
and drank port wine
from half-gallon jugs

kept the chain on the
door
windows boarded

you had to give
a special knock
to get in

he had brass knucks
knives
clubs
guns

he had a chest like a
wrestler
never lost his
glasses

never swore
never looked for
trouble

never married after the death
of his only
wife

hated
cats
roaches
mice
humans

worked crossword
puzzles
kept up with the
news

that 16 and one-half inch
neck

for 68 he was
something

all those boards
across the windows

washed his own underwear
and socks

my friend Red took me up
to meet him
one night

we talked a while
together

then we left

Red asked, "what do you
think?"

I answered, "more afraid to die
than the rest of us."

I haven't seen either of them
since.

the sandwich

I walked down the street for a submarine
sandwich
and this guy pulled out of the driveway
of The Institute of Sexual Education
and almost ran over my toes
with his bike;
he had a black dirty beard
eyes like a Russian pianist
and the breath of an East Kansas City whore;
it irritated me to be almost murdered by a
fool in a sequin jacket;
I looked upstairs and the girls sat in their chairs
outside their doors
dreaming old Greta Garbo movies;
I put a half a buck into one of the paper racks
and got the latest sex paper;
then I went into the sandwich shop
and ordered the submarine
and a large coffee.
they were all sitting in there talking about
how to lose weight.
I asked for a sideorder of
french fries.
the girls in the sex paper ads
looked like girls in sex paper ads.
they told me not to be lonely
that they could fix me up:
I could beat them with chains or whips
or they could beat me
with chains or whips, whichever way
I wanted it.
I finished, paid up, left a tip,
left the sex paper on the seat.
then I walked back up Western Avenue
with my belly hanging out over
my belt.

the happy life of the tired

neatly in tune with
the song of a fish
I stand in the kitchen
halfway to madness
dreaming of Hemingway's
Spain.
it's muggy, like they say,
I can't breathe,
have crapped and
read the sports pages,
opened the refrigerator
looked at a piece of purple
meat,
tossed it back
in.

the place to find the center
is at the edge
that pounding in the sky
is just a water pipe
vibrating.

terrible things inch in the
walls; cancer flowers grow
on the porch; my white cat has
one eye torn
away and there are only 7 days
of racing left in the
summer meet.

the dancer never arrived from the
Club Normandy
and Jimmy didn't bring the
hooker,
but there's a postcard from
Arkansas

and a throwaway from Food King:
10 free vacations to Hawaii,
all I got to do is
fill out the form.
but I don't want to go to
Hawaii.

I want the hooker with the pelican eyes
brass belly-button
and
ivory heart.

I take out the piece of purple
meat
drop it into the
pan.

then the phone rings.

I fall to one knee and roll under the
table. I remain there
until it
stops.

then I get up and
turn on the
radio.
no wonder Hemingway was a
drunk, Spain be damned,
I can't stand it
either.

it's so
muggy.

the proud
thin
dying

I see old people on pensions in the
supermarkets and they are thin and they are
proud and they are dying
they are starving on their feet and saying
nothing. long ago, among other lies,
they were taught that silence was
bravery. now, having worked a lifetime,
inflation has trapped them. they look around
steal a grape
chew on it. finally they make a tiny
purchase, a day's worth.
another lie they were taught:
thou shalt not steal.
they'd rather starve than steal
(one grape won't save them)
and in tiny rooms
while reading the market ads
they'll starve
they'll die without a sound
pulled out of roominghouses
by young blond boys with long hair
who'll slide them in
and pull away from the curb, these
boys
handsome of eye
thinking of Vegas and pussy and
victory.
it's the order of things: each one
gets a taste of honey
then the knife.

under

I can't pick anything up
off the floor—
old socks
shorts
shirts
newspapers
letters
spoons   bottles   beercaps

can't make the bed
hang up the toilet paper
brush my teeth
comb my hair
dress

I stay on the bed
naked
on the soiled sheets
which are half on the
floor
the buttons on the mattress
press into my
back

when the phone rings
when somebody comes to the door
I anger

I'm like a bug under a rock
with that fear too

I stay in bed
notice the mirror on the dresser

it is a victory to scratch
myself.

hot month

got 3 women coming down in
July, maybe more
they want to suck my blood-
vibes

do I have enough
clean towels?

I told them that I was feeling
bad
(I didn't expect all these
mothers
arriving with their tits
distended)

you see
I am too good
with the drunken letter
and the drunken phonecall
screaming for love
when I probably don't
have it

I am going out to buy more
towels
bedsheets
Alka-Seltzer
washrags
mop handles
mops
swords
knives
bombs
vaseline flowers of yearning
the works of
De Sade.

maybe tomorrow

looked like
>   Bogart
sunken cheeks

chain smoker

pissed out of windows
ignored women

snarled at landlords

rode boxcars through the badlands

never missed a chance to duke it

full of roominghouse and skidrow stories

ribs showing

flat belly

walking in shoes with nails driving into his heels

looking out of windows

cigar in mouth
lips wet with beer

>   Bogart's
got a beard now

he's much older

but don't believe the gossip:
>   Bogie's not dead
yet.

junk

sitting in a dark bedroom with 3 junkies,
female.
brown paper bags filled with trash are
everywhere.
it is one-thirty in the afternoon.
they talk about madhouses,
hospitals.
they are waiting for a fix.
none of them work.
it's relief and foodstamps and
Medi-Cal.

men are usable objects
toward the fix.

it is one-thirty in the afternoon
and outside small plants grow.
their children are still in school.
the females smoke cigarettes
and suck listlessly on beer and
tequila
which I have purchased.

I sit with them.
I wait on my fix:
I am a poetry junkie.

they pulled Ezra through the streets
in a wooden cage.
Blake was sure of God.
Villon was a mugger.
Lorca sucked cock.
T. S. Eliot worked a teller's cage.

most poets are swans,
egrets.

I sit with 3 junkies
at one-thirty in the afternoon.

the smoke pisses upward.

I wait.

death is a nothing jumbo.

one of the females says that she likes
my yellow shirt.

I believe in a simple violence.

this is
some of it.

8 rooms

my dentist is a drunk.
he rushes into the room while I'm
having my teeth cleaned:
"hey, you old fuck! you still
writing dirty stories?"
"yes."
he looks at the nurse:
"me and this old fuck, we both used
to work for the post office down at
the terminal annex!"
the nurse doesn't answer.
"look at us now! we got *out* of
there; we got out of that place,
didn't we?"
"yes, yes . . ."
he runs off into another room.
he hires beautiful young girls,
they are everywhere.
they work a 4 day week and he drives
a yellow Caddy.
he has 8 rooms besides the waiting
room, all equipped.
the nurse presses her body against
mine. it's unbelievable
her breasts, her thighs, her body
press against me. she picks at my teeth
and looks into my eyes:
"am I hurting you?"
"no no, go ahead!"

in 15 minutes the dentist is back:
"hey, don't take too long!
what's going on, anyhow?"
"Dr., this man hasn't had his teeth
cleaned for 5 years. they're filthy!"
"all right, finish him off! give him

104

another appointment!"
he runs out.
"would you like another appointment?"
she looks into my eyes.
"yes," I tell her.
she lets her body fall full against mine
and gives me a few last scrapes.
the whole thing only costs me forty dollars
including x-rays.

but she never told me her
name.

I liked him

I liked D. H. Lawrence
he could get so indignant
he snapped and he ripped
with wonderfully energetic sentences
he could lay the word down
bright and writhing
there was the stink of blood and murder
and sacrifice about him
the only tenderness he allowed
was when he bedded down his large German
wife.
I liked D. H. Lawrence—
he could talk about Christ
like he was the man next door
and he could describe Australian taxi drivers
so well you hated them
I liked D. H. Lawrence
but I'm glad I never met him
in some bistro
him lifting his tiny hot cup of
tea
and looking at me
with his worm-hole eyes.

106

the killer smiles

the old girl friends still phone
some from last year
some from the year before
some from the years before that.
it's good to have things done with
when they don't work
it's also good not to hate
or even forget
the person you've failed
with.

and I like it when they tell me
they are having luck with a man
luck with their life.

after surviving me
they have many joys due them.
I make their lives seem better
after me.

now I have given them
comparisons
new horizons
new cocks
more peace
a good future
without me.

I always hang up,
justified.

horse and fist

boxing matches and the racetracks
are where the guts are extracted and
rubbed into the cement
into the substance and stink of
being.

there is no peace either for the
flower or the tiger.
that's obvious.

what is not obvious are the rules.
there are no rules.

some attempt to find rules in the teachings of
others
and adjust to that
sight.

for me
obedience to another is the decay
of self.

for though every being is similar
each being is different

and to herd our differences
under one law
degrades each
self.

the boxing matches and the racetracks are
temples of learning

as the same horse and the same man
do not always win or lose
for the same reason

so does learning
sometimes
stand still
pause or
reverse itself.

there are very very
few
guidelines.

no rules
but a hint:

watch for the lead right
and the last flash of the
tote.

close encounters of another kind

are we going to the movies or not?
she asked him.

all right, he said, let's go.

I'm not going to put any panties on
so you can finger-fuck me in the
dark, she said.

should we get buttered popcorn?
he asked.

sure, she said.

leave your panties on,
he said.

what is it? she asked.

I just want to watch the movie,
he answered.

look, she said, I could go out on
the street, there are a hundred men
out there who'd be delighted to have
me.

all right, he said, go ahead out there.
I'll stay home and read the *National
Enquirer.*

you son of a bitch, she said, I am
trying to build a meaningful
relationship.

you can't build it with a hammer,
he said.

are we going to the movies or not?
she asked.

all right, he said, let's
go . . .

at the corner of Western and
Franklin he put on the blinker
to make his left turn
and a man in the on-coming lane
speeded-up
as if to cut him off.

brakes grabbed. there wasn't a
crash but there almost was one.

he cursed at the man in the other
car. the man cursed back. the
man had another person in the car with
him. it was *his* wife.

they were going to the movies
too.

mermaid

I had to come to the bathroom for something
and I knocked
and you were in the tub
you had washed your face and your hair
and I saw your upper body
and except for the breasts
you looked like a girl of 5, of 8
you were gently gleeful in the water
Linda Lee.
you were not only the essence of that
moment
but of all my moments
up to then
you bathing easily in the ivory
yet there was nothing
I could tell you.

I got what I wanted in the bathroom
something
and I left.

hug the dark

turmoil is the god
madness is the god

permanent living peace is
permanent living death.

agony can kill
or
agony can sustain life
but peace is always horrifying
peace is the worst thing
walking
talking
smiling,
seeming to be.

don't forget the sidewalks
the whores,
betrayal,
the worm in the apple,
the bars, the jails,
the suicides of lovers.

here in America
we have assassinated a president and his brother,
another president has quit office.

people who believe in politics
are like people who believe in god:
they are sucking wind through bent
straws.

there is no god
there are no politics
there is no peace
there is no love

there is no control
there is no plan

stay away from god
remain disturbed

slide.

59 cents a pound

I like to prowl ordinary places
and taste the people—
from a distance.
I don't want them too near
because that's when attrition
starts.
but in supermarkets
laundromats
cafés
street corners
bus stops
eating places
drug stores
I can look at their bodies
and their faces
and their clothing—
watch the way they walk
or stand
or what they are doing.
I'm like an x-ray machine
I like them like that:
on view.
I imagine the best things
about them.
I imagine them brave and crazy
I imagine them beautiful.

I like to prowl the ordinary places.
I feel sorry for us all or glad for us
all
caught alive together
and awkward in that way.

there's nothing better than the joke
of us
the seriousness of us
the dullness of us

buying stockings and carrots and gum
and magazines
buying birth control
candy
hair spray
and toilet paper.

we should build a great bonfire
we should congratulate ourselves on our
endurance

we stand in long lines
we walk about
we wait.

I like to prowl ordinary places
the people explain themselves to me
and I to them

a woman at 3:35 p.m.
weighing purple grapes on a scale
looking at that scale very
seriously
she is dressed in a simple green dress
with a pattern of white flowers
she takes the grapes
puts them carefully into a white paper
bag

that's lightning enough

the generals and the doctors may kill us
but we have
won.

promenade

each night
well, almost every night
early in the evening
I see the old man
and his small black and white dog.
it's dark on these streets
and no matter how often he has seen me
he always gives me
a look that is frightened
and yet bold—
bold because his small brittle dog is
with him.
he wears old clothing
a wrinkled cap
cotton gloves
large square-toed shoes.
we never speak.
he is my age but I feel younger.
I neither like nor dislike the man and his
dog.
I have never seen either of them
defecate but I know that they
must.
he and his dog give me a feeling of
peace.
they belong
like the street signs
the lawns
the yellow windows
the sidewalks
the sirens and the telephone
wires.
the driveways
the parked cars
the moon when there is a
moon.

117

metamorphosis

a girlfriend came in
built me a bed
scrubbed and waxed the kitchen floor
scrubbed the walls
vacuumed
cleaned the toilet
the bathtub
scrubbed the bathroom floor
and cut my toenails and
my hair.

then
all on the same day
the plumber came and fixed the kitchen faucet
and the toilet
and the gas man fixed the heater
and the phone man fixed the phone.
now I sit here in all this perfection.
it is quiet.
I have broken off with all 3 of my girlfriends.

I felt better when everything was in
disorder.
it will take me some months to get back to
normal:
I can't even find a roach to commune with.

I have lost my rhythm.
I can't sleep.
I can't eat.

I have been robbed of
my filth.

we'll take them

those lobsters
those 2 lobsters . . .
yes, those bastards there.
we'll take them . . .

so pink-red.

they say if you put them
in warm water first
they'll sleep
and when you boil them
they won't feel it.

how can we know?

no matter the burning tanks outside
Stalingrad
no matter that Hitler was a
vegetarian
no matter that the house I was born in
is now a brothel
in Andernach
no matter that my Uncle Heinrich
aged 92 and living in that same town
dislikes my novels and short stories.

we'll take those 2
bastards there

flowers of the sea.

dow average down

when you
first meet them their eyes
are all under-
standing; laughter abounds
like sand fleas. then, Je-
sus, time tinkles on and
things leak. they
start making DEMANDS.
what they
demand is contrary to what-
ever you are, or could be.
strange is the
thought that they've never
read anything you've writ-
ten, not really read it at
all. or worse, if they have,
they've come to SAVE
you. which mainly means
making you like everybody
else. meanwhile they've sucked
you up and wound you tight
in a million webs, and
being something of a
feeling person you can't
help but remember the
good parts or the parts
that *seemed* to be good.

you find yourself
alone again in your
bedroom grabbing your
guts and saying, o, shit
no, not again.

we should have known.
maybe we wanted cotton

candy luck. maybe we
believed. what trash.
we believed like dogs
believe.

to weep

sweating in the kitchen
trying to hit one out of here
56 years old
fear bounding up my arms
toenails much too long
growth on side of leg

the difference in the factories was
we all felt pain
together

the other night I went to see the
great soprano
she was still beautiful
still sensual
still in personal mourning
but she missed note after note
drunk
she murdered art

sweating in the kitchen
I don't want to murder art

I should see the doctor and get that thing
cut off my leg
but I am a coward
I might scream and frighten a child
in the waiting room

I would like to fuck the great soprano
I'd like to weep in her hair

and there's Lorca down in the road
eating Spanish bullets in the dust

the great soprano has never read my poems
but we both know how to murder art
drink and mourn

sweating in this kitchen
the formulas are gone
the best poet I ever knew is dead
the others write me letters

I tell them that I want to fuck
the great soprano
but they write back about other
things
useless things
dull things
vain things

I watch a fly land on my radio

he knows what it is
but he can't talk to me

the soprano is dead.

fair stand the fields of France

in the awesome strumming of no
guitars
I can never get too high

in places where giraffes run like
hate
I can never get too lonely

in bars where celluloid bartenders
serve poisoned laughter
I can never get too drunk

at the bottom of mountains
where suicides flow into the streams
I smile better than the Mona Lisa

high lonely drunken grin of grief
I love you.

art

as the
spirit
wanes
the
form
appears.

Photo: Richard Robinson

ecco

An Imprint of HarperCollinsPublishers
www.harpercollins.com

www.ingramcontent.com/pod-product-compliance
Lightning Source LLC
LaVergne TN
LVHW030715100225
803315LV00004B/14